THE GOLDADE
FAMILY HISTORY

OTHER WORKS BY THE AUTHOR

The Goldade Family History with Memories of the Village Selz.
The Sander Family History with Memories of the Village Selz.
The Jundt Family History with Memories of the Village Selz.
The Migler Family History.
Our Relatives the Persecuted.
Life Under Tyranny

THE GOLDADE FAMILY HISTORY

- SECOND EDITION

PETER GOLDADE

Library of Congress Control Number: 2023905549
ISBN: Hardcover   978-1-6698-7168-2
                     Softcover   978-1-6698-7167-5
                     eBook   978-1-6698-7166-8

Print information available on the last page.

Rev. date: 03/22/2023

To order additional copies of this book, contact:
Xlibris
844-714-8691
www.Xlibris.com
Orders@Xlibris.com
851311

Contents

The Cover...vii

Dedication..ix

Acknowledgments...xi

Note xiii

Chapter 1 Johann Joseph Goldate/Goldade............................... 1

Chapter 2 Anton Goldate... 5

Chapter 3 Stephan Goldade 9

Chapter 4 Goldade/Goldate Ancestral Chart............................17

Chapter 5 The Gottlieb Goldade Ancestral Chart 23

Chapter 6 The Reiss Family ancestral chart 29

Chapter 7 Johannes Goldade Family story 39

List of Germans who resided in Ulitino in the 1940's – 1950's................. 56

The Cover

The iron cross grave marker was a trademark of early the German-Russians who settled in the U. S. The crosses were produced by foundries and also by local blacksmiths. The foundries produced several styles of the crosses, while the local blacksmith used his own resources in the design.

The cross on the cover is that of the author's uncle Balthasar Goldade's grave, located in the Odessa cemetery, in Benson County, North Dakota.

Dedication

To all of the ethnic Germans who were living in Russia, who were so ruthlessly displaced, send to labor and resettlement camps, where they suffered and many died at the hands of their Russian Captors.

Acknowledgments

A special thanks to Sergey and Mila Koretnikov for finding the book *Proceedings of Vologda Society for Northern Region Studies*, which helped me to locate the family of my relative Johannes Goldade and locating the author Ms. Ludmila Mutovkina.

A special thanks to Ms. Ludmila Mutovkina, who as a high student wrote a spectacular article on the ethnic Germans who were living in a resettlement camp in Russia and granting me permission to reprint the article.

Note

This book <u>does not</u> replace my original book, The Goldade Family History with Memories of the Village Selz. This book will clarify and correct several entries in the original book. The clarifications and corrections are the result of some newly found documents.

Chapter 1

Johann Joseph Goldate/Goldade

Our ancestor – my great great grandfather, Johann Joseph Goldade was born on 25 February 1788 in the village of Jockgrim, Germany. Johann Joseph was the son of Johann Sebastian and Margaretha (nee Kimmel(er) Goldate. Unfortunately, we have not found any information relating to Johann Joseph in his early years.

The earliest information, that we have for Johann Joseph is his immigration to Russia in 1809. In 1804 Czar Alexander I repeated the earlier manifesto issued by his grandmother Catherine the Great, inviting Germans to Russia. Johann Joseph along with many other people responded to the invitation.

Karl Stumpp, in his book *The Emigration from Germany to Russia in the Years 1763 – 1862*, lists Johann Joseph and his wife Margaretha as original settlers of the Black Sea Kutschurgan village of Selz. In his book *Auswanderer Aus Jockgrim Im 19 Jahrhundert* Hans Rasimus, also states that Johann Joseph Goldate and his wife Margaretha nee Keiber immigrated to Russia in 1809. Hans Rasimus further states that Margaretha Keiber was born on 17 August 1783 and was the daughter of Johann Albert and Anna Maria (nee Fahn) Keiber. However, Hans Rasimus goes on to state that he did not find a marriage record for Johann Joseph Goldate and Margaretha Keiber. In my many years of Goldate research, I also have not found a marriage record for Johann Joseph and Margaretha.

In 2019 I had the pleasure of making contact with a Mr. Peter Distl of Jockgrim, Germany. Mr. Distl is a renowned; researcher, Bibliographer and

Author. Mr. Distl published his book *Ortsfamilienbuch Jockgrim 1684 – 1909* in 2019.

Mr. Distl states that there are no civil or church documents, stating that Johann Joseph and Margaretha were ever married. His conclusion is that Johann Joseph and Margaretha simply traveled to Russia as an unmarried couple.

In my research of Johann Joseph in the early years in Russia, I recovered a file from the Odessa State Archive, which stated that Johann Joseph was gone from the village of Selz for a portion of the year of 1810. What did Johann Joseph do during his absence from Selz in 1810? Did he escort Margaretha Keiber to a different destination? Another file which I recovered from the Odessa State Archive, was titled 1811 civil marriages. This document states that in May of 1811 Johann Joseph married Margaretha Becker. Margaretha was born on 15 June 1793, near Busenbach, Baden, Germany. She was the daughter of Johann Georg and Maria Anna (nee Schneider) Becker. The file does not list Johann Joseph as a widower at the time of this marriage. The conclusion is that Johann Joseph had not been married to Margaretha Keiber and his marriage to Margaretha Becker was his first marriage.

The question remains, why did Johann Joseph Goldate and Margaretha Keiber travel to Russia as a couple and how did they benefit from the pretense that they were married. In the case of Johann Joseph, it appears that he gained all of the benefits of the Manifesto, which included land. The Manifesto stated that the benefits were for families, which implies that people should have been married. As for Margaretha Keiber, it appears that she got a ticket to her desired destination in Eastern Europe. Her fate beyond this point is unknown.

Some researchers had speculated, that Johann Joseph had taken Margaretha Keiber back to Jockgrim. However, Mr. Distl refutes this theory, as there are no documents relating to a Margaretha Keiber born 07 August 1783 in Jockgrim after her departure for Russia in 1809. Adding to the confusion on the fate of Margaretha Keiber who was born on 07 August 1783 is the fact, that the father Johann Albert Keiber had a second daughter with the name of Margaretha. She was born on 26 October 1797. Each of these girls had the singular name of Margaretha and both reached adulthood.

I had relied on the Stumpp and Rasimus as sources for documentation of data and stated that Johann Joseph Goldate and Margaretha Keiber were married, which we now have concluded, that it was an error.

"Government is not the solution to the problem; Government is the problem."

Ronald Reagan

Chapter 2

Anton Goldate

The person referenced here is Anton Goldate born on 5 September 1716, he was the son of Simon and Maria Magdalena (née Scherer) Goldate. In my original book *The Goldade Family History*, I show Anton married to Maria Elisabetha Gortner. This is erroneous. Anton was really married to Maria Elisabetha Marmuth. Maria Elisabetha Marmuth was born on 29 February 1720 and was the daughter of Johann Georg and Apolonia (née Schoss) Marmuth.

In my early research of the Goldate family, we were unable to locate an official marriage record for Anton and Maria Elisabetha. Along with some fellow researchers, we relied on various Jockgrim village documents for their marriage. The problem was that some documents had Anton married to Maria Elisabetha Gortner and other documents had him married to Maria Elisabetha Marmuth. We were aware, that there were some scribe entry errors on these documents. Since we had to rely on the few available documents, all indications were that Anton had married Maria Elisabetha Gortner. This is an example, that without an official record, secondary documents can be wrong. In recent years the official marriage records for that period have been recovered, and we now with certainty know that Anton married Maria Elisabetha Marmuth. The following document is one example of several conflicting documents regarding the marriage of Anton Goldate. The scribe errors in this document show that Anton had children with Maria Elisabeth Gortner and Maria Elisabetha Marmuth, which did not happen.

LDS FILM No. 008232530 pg. 33

	Namen		der Ältern			Nation der Ältern	Pathen des Vaters		der Mutter		Bemerkung
			Jahr	Monat	Tag						
12	Goldade	Franz	1789	Juli	17	Geburt Akt	Goldade	Georg Wendelin	Gordner	Anna Maria	
9	.	G. Peter	1791	März	10	. Akt			.	.	
13	.	Gg. Anton	1746	Juni	20	. Akt		Anton	.	Mar. [illegible]	
22	.	Margaretha	1748	Dezem.	1	. Akt			.	.	
13	.	Gg. Wendelin	1751	Mai	31	. Akt			.	.	
4	.	Jof. Sebastian	1755	Februar	16	. Akt			.	.	
21	.	Gg. Adam	1742	Novem.	17	. Akt			Marmuth	.	
6	.	Jof. Jacob	1759	Mai	23	. Akt			.	.	
27	.	Gg. Nicolaus	1769	Novem.	19	. Akt		Gg. Anton	.	Mar. [illegible]	
22	.	Jof. Christof	1772	Oktober	6	. Akt			Becker	.	
19	.	Anna Maria	1775	Juli	11	. Akt			.	.	
13	.	Gg. Anton	1775	.	16	. Akt			.	.	
5	.	G. Anton	1781	Februar	7	. Akt			.	.	
16	.	Mar. Anna	1753	Januar	26	. Akt			.	.	
37	.	Mar. Catharina	1757	Oktober	16	. Akt			.	.	

Jockgrim Family village listing for the family of Anton Goldate
Anton born 12 Sept. 1716 Jockgrim.

The listing of the children born to Anton is correct.
Johann Adam born 17 Nov. 1742.
Georg Anton born 20 June 1746.
Margaretha born 01 Dec. 1748.
Georg Wendelin born 31 May 1751.
Johann Sebastian born 16 Feb. 1755.
Johann Jacob born 23 May 1759

However, the record has a scribe entry error, as it states the mother of the children: Georg Anton, Margaretha, Georg Wendelin and Johann Sebastian was a Maria Elisabetha Gortner. This incorrect as Anton was only married to Maria Elisabetha Marmet/Marmuth.

The following is the marriage record for Anton Goldate and Maria Elisabetha Marmuth. Married on 6 February 1741 in Jockgrim. Anton Goldate born 12 September 1716 in Jockgrim. Maria Elisabetha Marmuth born on February 1720 in Worth, Palatinate, Germany.

Family listing book of marriages LDS film # 008232530 page 134

*The citizen who sees his society's
democratic clothes being worn out and does
not cry it out, is not a patriot, but a traitor.*

Mark Twain

Chapter 3

Stephan Goldade

In the early years of my research, church records were not yet available for the early German settlers in Russia. Therefore, we had to rely on civil records. Early civil records, such as family listings and census for the Kutschurgan village of Selz had a Stephan Goldade living in the same house as Johann Joseph Goldade. The assumption was, that Stephan was the son of Johann Joseph. This was most logical, as the Johann Joseph Goldade family, was the only known Goldade family living in the Odessa region of Russia. These early civil records indicated that Stephan was born about 1814. Since Johann Joseph was married in 1811, this fit for Stephan to be his eldest child. As convincing as they were, relying on these civil records for the father of Stephan Goldade being Johann Joseph Goldade was an error.

Among my early sources for researching the Goldate family, was the book *Auswanderer Aus Jockgrim Im 19 Jahrhundert* by Hans Rasimus. In his book Hans Rasimus states, that the brother Johannes to Johann Joseph Goldate and his family also immigrated to Russia in 1819. The family of Johannes consisted of his wife Anna Maria and their sons Georg Michael and Stephan. Johannes was born on 25 August 1782 in Jockgrim. Anna Maria was the daughter of Kasper and Catharina (née Straus) Keiber and was born on 10 March 1782. Johannes and Anna Maria were married on 12 June 1811. Their son Stephan was born on 15 March 1814 and son Georg Michael on 3 September 1818.

Allegedly, Johannes had made a statement to family and friends in Jockgrim that he was going to the village of Krim in Russia. To date we have not been able to identify a Russian village with name of Krim. However, the

Russian name for Crimea was Krim. Therefore, it is a possibility that Johannes settled in Crimea. I have only found one document in the Odessa State Archive, which relates to Johannes's immigration to Russia. The document was Johannes's passport check point registration in Odessa. At this station Johannes made the statement that he was 'going east'. East of Odessa is a very large area.

Since Johannes Goldate and his family did not remain in the Odessa region, it left the Johann Joseph Goldate family as the only Goldate/Goldade family in the Odessa region. Therefore, the assumption was mas made, that all Goldate/Goldade members living with the Johann Joseph Goldate/Goldade family were members of that family.

Thanks to the determination and dedication to the researchers with the Germans from Russia Heritage Society, who continue to retrieve all of the available Catholic Church records for the Kutschurgan villages. This past year the group retrieved the marriage record for Stephan Goldade. The record states that on 20 September 1836 Stephan Goldade, at the age of 22 married Genevieva Thomas, she the age of 19. The record goes on to state that Stephan was the son of Johannes and Anna Maria (née Keiber) Goldade and, that Genevieva Thomas was the daughter of Wilhelm and Anna Maria (nee Doll) Thomas.

Apparently, shortly after arriving in Russia, Johannes Goldate died. The widow, Anna Maria (née Keiber) Goldate, then placed her son Stephan in the care of his uncle Johann Joseph Goldate. This would explain the reason that the civil records for that period show Stephan living in the household of Johann Joseph Goldate.

The group retrieved an additional record for this family, it was the death record for Anna Maria (née Keiber) Goldate. The record states that Anna Maria died on 6 May 1835 in the Kutschurgan village of Selz. At the time of her death, Anna Maria's married name was Bertram.

The marriage record for Anna Maria and Peter Bertram has not been recovered.

Stephan Goldade Family Group Sheet

Subject: Stephan Goldade (184)
Birth*   15 Mar. 1814 Jockgrim, Germany.

Marriage*   20 Sept. 1836 Selz, Kutschurgan, Odessa, Russia.

Death*   19 Feb. 1880 Selz, Kutschurgan, Odessa, Russia.

Father*   Johannes Goldate (180) (b. 25 Aug. 1782),

Mother*   Anna Maria Keiber (181) (b. 10 Mar. 1782, d. 6 May 1835

Spouse*   Genevieva Thomas (185)

Birth*   Circa __ ___ 1817 Selz, Kutschurgan, Odessa, Russia.

Marr. Name- Goldade

Marr: 20 Sept. 1836

Death*   11 July 1895 Selz, Kutschurgan, Odessa, Russia.

Father*   Wilhelm Thomas (4039)

Mother*   Anna Maria Herrle (4040)

Ten Known Children

1). M. Georg Goldade (309)
     Birth* 7 Sept. 1838 Selz, Kutschurgan, Odessa, Russia.
     Death 9 Jan. 1913 Hague, North Dakota
     Marriage* 26 Oct. 1859 Marianna Lipp (315) (b. 15 Feb. 1841, d. 2
Jan. 1934), daughter of Joseph Lipp (4034) and Elisabetha Tersam (4035);
Selz, Russia.

2). F Anna Maria Goldade (310)
     Birth* 30 Mar. 1842 Selz, Kutschurgan, Odessa, Russia.
     Death 14 June 1873 Selz, Kutschurgan, Odessa, Russia
     Marriage* 07 Nov. 1860 Leonhard Joachim

3). F. Beathrice Goldade (550)
     Birth* 06 Nov. 1844 Selz, Russia.
     Death 21 Sept. 1925
     Marriage* __ ___ Georg Deibert (3607)

4). F. Rosalia Goldade (311)
     Birth* 6 June 1847 Selz, Kutschurgan, Odessa, Russia.
     Death* 6 June 1847 Selz, Kutschurgan, Odessa, Russia.

5). F. Margaretha Goldade (312)

    Birth* 23 Dec. 1849 Selz, Kutschurgan, Odessa, Russia.

    Marriage* 24 Oct. 1871 Joseph Weiss (1022) (b. 1 Jue 1852), son of Karl Weiss (1313) and Elisabeth Degenstein (1314)

6). M. Johannes Goldade (202)

    Birth* 9 Mar. 1852 Selz, Kutschurgan, Odessa, Russia.

    Death 9 Nov. 1935 Emmons County, North Dakota

    Marriage* 21 Apr. 1877 Johanna Reiss (201) (b. 9 Nov. 1857, d. 10 July 1929), daughter of Johannes Joseph Reiss (18) and Barbara Sander (19); Selz, Russia.

7). M. Jacob Goldade (313)

    Birth* 25 Mar. 1855 Selz, Kutschurgan, Odessa, Russia.

    Death 19 Sept. 1928 Beulah, North Dakota

    Marriage* 29 Apr. 1877 Margaretha Fetsch (316); Selz, Kutschgan, Russia.

8). F. Marion Goldade (321)

    Birth* circa __ 1856 Selz, Kutschurgan, Odessa, Russia.

9). F. Elisabetha Goldade (4054)

    Birth* 9 Aug. 1837 Selz, Kutschurgan, Odessa, Russia.

    Death* 30 Oct. 1838 Selz, Kutschurgan, Odessa, Russia

10). F Rosalia Goldade (314)

    Birth* 3 Jan. 1859 Selz, Kutschurgan, Odessa, Russia.

    Death 8 Dec. 1941 Bismarck, North Dakota

    Marriage* 26 Nov. 1878 Wendelin Zahn (322) (b. 9 May 1851, d. 16 Jul 1921); Selz, Kutschurgan, Odessa, Russia

Printed on: 19 Jan. 2023

Prepared by: P. Goldade

4 generation ancestral chart for
Stephan Goldate/Goldade

1ˢᵗ generation

1). Stephan Goldade (184) was born 15 March 1814 at Jockgrim, Germany. He married Genevieva Thomas (185) daughter of Wilhelm Thomas (4039) and Anna Maria Herrle (4040), on 20 September 1836 at Selz, Kutshurgan, Russia. He died on 19 February 1880 at Selz, Kutschurgan, Russia, at the age of 65.

2ⁿᵈ generation

2). Johannes Goldate (180) was born on 25 August 1782 at Jockgrim, Germany. He married Anna Maria Keiber (181) daughter of Casper Keiber (4043) and Catharina Strauss (4044), on 2 June 1811 at Jockgrim, Germany. He immigrated in 1819 from Jockgrim, Germany, to Russia.

3ʳᵈ generation

3). Johann Sebastian Goldate (32) was born 16 February 1755 at Jockgrim, Germany. He married Margaretha Kimmel(er) (33) on 9 May 1779 at Jockgrim, Germany. He died after 1789 at Jockgrim, Germany.

4ᵗʰ generation

4). Anton Goldate (54) was born on 5 September 1716 at Jockgrim, Germany. He married Maria Elisabetha Marmuth (55), daughter of Johann Georg Mamuth (4048) and Apolonia Schoss (4049), on 6 February 1741 at Jockgrim, Germany. He died circa 1762 at Jockgrim, Germany.

Printed on 19 Jan. 2023
Prepared by: P. Goldade

My original book *The Goldade Family History with Memories of the village Selz*, contains some additional information for the Stephan Goldade family.

Copies of the marriage record of Stephan Goldade with Genevieva Thomas and the death record of Anna Maria (nee Keiber) – Goldade – Bertram, can be purchased from the Germans from Russia Heritage Society (GRHS) of Bismarck, North Dakota

"I've learned that from a war ignited by revenge, nothing can be born."

Shinobu Ohtak

Chapter 4

Goldade/Goldate Ancestral Chart

Here we have the current Goldade/Goldate/Goldader family ancestral chart. We are convinced, that this is a complete and accurate chart. I started the chart with Anton Goldade born on 25 November 1838. The reason that I selected this Anton for the base of the chart, is that this is the most convenient point for any Goldade/Goldate/Goldader individual to identify their ancestor and complete their personal ancestral chart.

The only differences to this and my previous charts, is the corrected marriage of Anton Goldade to Maria Elisabetha Marmuth and the addition of an additional ancestor Anton Goldate. This Anton is the father of the Anton born circa 1625 and died on 18 Jan. 1690.

Additionally, we now also know that the Anton who was born about 1625 and died on 18 January 1690 was married twice. The name of his first wife was Eulesia Chesaurarus. The children of that marriage were, Anton born about 1666 and Anna Barbara born about 1667. (Anna Barbara married Johann Wilhelm Gebhart).

A few interesting points of our ancestry. Prior to about 1650 the family name was Gold, at times it was also spelled as Goll. About 1650 our ancestor Anton who was born about 1625 decided to change the name. There is a document which shows a few variants of Anton's proposed new family name. It was then that Anton decided on using the name Gold-ate.

In German 'ate' has no definitive meaning. However, in French 'ate' in general could mean Adieu or goodbye. Since Jockgrim is located right on the Rhine River bordering France, Anton could have had some French influence.

Later when our ancestor immigrated to Russia, the spelling of the name changed from Gold-ate to Gold-ade. I have not found an explanation for this change. In a more current setting, one family who settled in Bismarck, North Dakota added an 'r' to the name for Goldader.

Thus, as we have moved through history, we have the known family name from Gold to Gold-ate and Gold-ade and Goldader.

Another interesting point was, many years ago, I participated in a DNA project. This DNA study followed Haplogroups. They concluded that at some point in history our ancestors had migrated through the area of Bosnia-Herzegovina and Croatia and later moved into the Tirol region. A common migration pattern in the early 1600s was movement from the Tirol region into the current area of Germany.

Pedigree

Chart #1

Chart of
Anton Goldade (8)

Cont.
2

Anton Goldate (54)

8
b. 5 Sep 1716
at Germany
d. circa 1782
at Germany
m. 6 Feb 1741
at Germany

Johann Sebastian Goldate (32)

4
b. 16 Feb 1755
at Germany
d. after 1789
at Germany
m. 9 May 1779
at Germany

Maria Elisabetha Marmuth (55)

9
b. 29 Feb 1720
at Germany
d.
at Germany

3

Johann Joseph Goldate (16)

2
b. 25 Feb 1788
at Germany
d. 1 Nov 1855
at Russia
m. May 1811
at Russia

Margaretha Kimmeler (33)

5
b. circa 1752
at Germany
d. after 1789
at Germany

Anton Goldade (8)

1
b. 25 Nov 1838
at Russia
d. 24 Dec 1889
at Russia
m. 19 Nov 1856
at Odessa, Russia

Magdalena Reiss (9)

SPOUSE
b. 13 Aug 1838
at Odessa, Russia
d. circa 1873
at Russia

Joseph Becker (3140)

12
b. 23 May 1719
at Germany
d. 1790
at Germany
m. 11 Jul 1739
at Germany

Johann Georg Becker (3085)

6
b. 10 Feb 1747
at Germany
d. 1815
at Russia
m. 17 Aug 1772
at Germany

Elisabetha Stäb (3141)

13
b. 5 Feb 1716
at Germany
d.
at

Margaretha Becker (697)

3
b. 16 Jun 1793
at Germany
d. 11 Nov 1856
at Russia

Anton Schneider (502)

14
b. 16 Jan 1716
at Baden, Germany
d. 5 Jun 1798
at Baden, Germany
m. 23 Nov 1739
at

Maria Anna Schneider (3050)

7
b. 29 Nov 1749
at Germany
d.
at

Anna Barbara Wirtheinz (503)

15
b. 3 Jan 1709
at Baden, Germany
d. 27 Mar 1777
at Baden, Germany

Printed on: 20 Jan 2023
Prepared by:
Peter Goldade

Pedigree

Chart #2

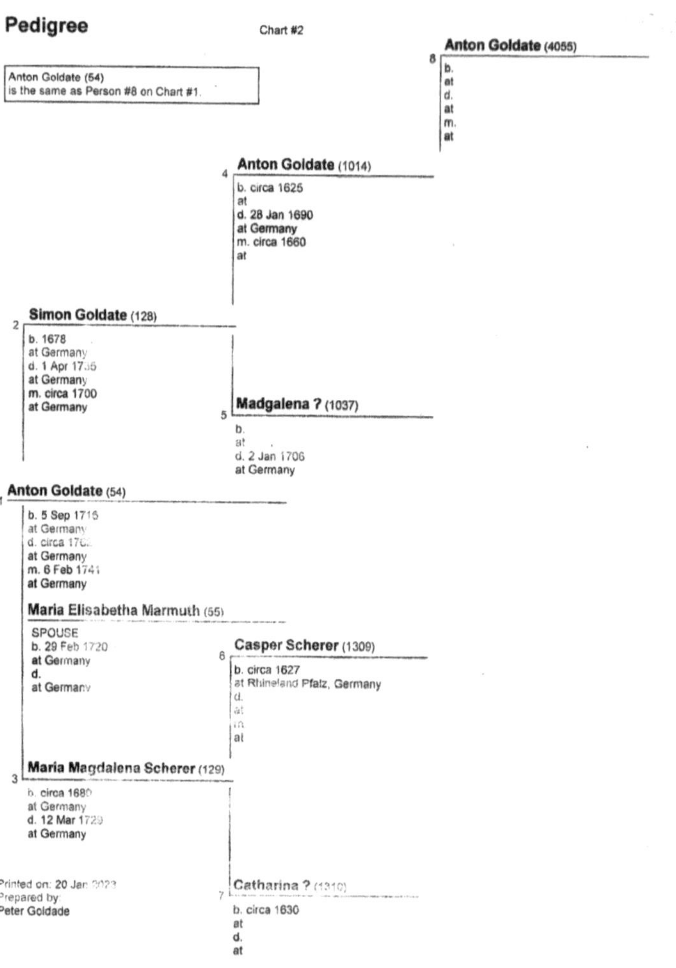

Anton Goldate (54)
is the same as Person #8 on Chart #1.

8   **Anton Goldate** (4055)
b.
at
d.
at
m.
at

4   **Anton Goldate** (1014)
b. circa 1625
at
d. 28 Jan 1690
at Germany
m. circa 1660
at

2   **Simon Goldate** (128)
b. 1678
at Germany
d. 1 Apr 1705
at Germany
m. circa 1700
at Germany

5   **Madgalena ?** (1037)
b.
at
d. 2 Jan 1706
at Germany

1   **Anton Goldate** (54)
b. 5 Sep 1715
at Germany
d. circa 1762
at Germany
m. 6 Feb 1741
at Germany

Maria Elisabetha Marmuth (55)
SPOUSE
b. 29 Feb 1720
at Germany
d.
at Germany

6   **Casper Scherer** (1309)
b. circa 1627
at Rhineland Pfalz, Germany
d.
at
m.
at

3   **Maria Magdalena Scherer** (129)
b. circa 1680
at Germany
d. 12 Mar 1729
at Germany

7   **Catharina ?** (1310)
b. circa 1630
at
d.
at

Printed on: 20 Jan 2023
Prepared by:
Peter Goldade

Pedigree

Chart #3

Maria Elisabetha Marmuth (55)
is the same as Person #9 on Chart #1.

4 **Christian Marmuth** (4051)
b.
at Württemburg, Germany
d.
at
m.
at

2 **Johann Georg Marmuth** (4048)
b.
at
d.
at
m.
at

5

1 **Maria Elisabetha Marmuth** (55)
b. 29 Feb 1720
at Germany
d.
at Germany
m. 6 Feb 1741
at Germany

Anton Goldate (54)
SPOUSE
b. 5 Sep 1716
at Germany
d. circa 1762
at Germany

6 **Johannes Jacob Schoss** (4050)
b.
at
d.
at
m.
at

3 **Apolonia Schoss** (4049)
b.
at
d.
at

Printed on: 20 Jan 2023
Prepared by:
Peter Goldade

"The problem with socialism is that you eventually run out of other peoples' money."

Margaret Thatcher

Chapter 5

The Gottlieb Goldade Ancestral Chart

The following is the ancestral chart for Gottlieb Goldade (my grandfather). The chart has one minor correction and one additional generation from the previous publications. This chart was previously published in my original book *The Goldade Family History with Memories of the Village Selz* and on my web site www.goldade.net

--- 1st Generation ---

1). Gottlieb Goldade (4) was born on 22 March 1865 at Selz, Odessa, Russia. He married Magdalena Jundt (5), daughter of Ignatius Jundt (10) and Maria Anna Riehl (11), on 8 October 1889 in Selz, Odessa, Russia. He emigrated on 13 November 1893. He was accepted for the homestead of 160 acres for a farm approximately 2.5 miles east and .5 miles south of Selz, North Dakota on 16 April 1897 at Devils Lake, North Dakota, USA. He was naturalized on 3 November 1900 at Rugby, North Dakota. He died on 17 February 1944 at Selz, Pierce Co., North Dakota at the age of 78.

--- 2nd Generation ---

2. Anton Goldade (8) was born on 25 November 1838 at Selz, Russia. He married Magdalena Reiss (9) daughter of Johannes Joseph Reiss (18) and Barbara Sander (19) on 19 November 1856 at Selz, Odessa, Russia. He married Valeria Schmidt (169) daughter of Johannes Nikolaus Schmidt

(170) and Lousia ? (1023) circa 1875 at Selz, Odessa, Russia. He died on 24 December 1889 at Meiorski, Russia.

--- 3 Generation ---

3. Johann Joseph Goldade (16) was born 25 February 1788 at Jockgrim, Germany. He and Margaretha Keiber (17) were engaged circa 1808. He emigrated in 1809. He married Margaretha Becker (697) the daughter of Johann Georg Becker (3085) and Maria Anna Schneider (3050), in May 1811 at Selz, Odessa, Russia. He died on 1 November 1855 at Selz, Odessa, Russia.

--- 4th Generation ---

4. Johann Sebastian Goldate (32) was born on 16 February 1755 at Jockrgim, Germany. He married Margaretha Kimmel(er) (33) on 9 May 1779 at Jockgim, Germany. He died after 1789 at Jockgrim, Germany.

--- 5th Generation ---

5. Anton Goldate (54) was born on 5 September 1716 at Jockgrim, Germany. He married Maria Elisabetha Marmuth (55) daughter of Johann Georg Marmuth (4048) and Apolonia Schoss (4049), on 6 February 1741 at Jockgrim, Germany. He died circa 1762 at Jockgrim, Germany.

--- 6th Generation ---

6. Simon Goldate (128) was born in1678 at Jockgrim, Germany. He married Maria Magdalena Scherer (129), daughter of Casper Scherer (1309) and Catharina ? (1310), circa 1700 at Jockgrim, Germany. He died on April 1735 at Jockgrim, Germany.

--- 7th Generation ---

7. Anton Goldate (1014) was born circa 1625. He married Eulesia Chesauarus (4056) circa 1650. He was Counsellor/Anwalt/Lawyer circa 1660 at Jockgrim, Germany. (Anton and Eulesia had son Anton and daughter Anna Barbara. Anna Barbara married Johann Wilhelm Gebhart). He married

Magdalena ? (1037) circa 1660. He died on 28 January 1690 at Jockgrim, Germany. (Anton and Magdalena had sons Johann Adam and Simon and daughter Margaretha. Margaretha married Johann Georg Bauer).

--- 8th Generation ---

8. Anton Goldate (4055) was born circa 1600.

Printed on 20 Feb. 2023 Prepared by: P. Goldade

*"Those who ignore history
are doomed to repeat it."*

George Santayana

CHAPTER 6

The Reiss Family ancestral chart

There are no additions or corrections to our ancestral Reiss family. This chart is a mirror reflection of all of the previous Reiss family charts that I have presented. Our Reiss ancestors, as our Goldade/Goldate ancestors originated from the Palatinate village of Jockgrim. The Goldate and Reiss families intermarried in Jockgrim and Russia. Therefore, it is fitting, that along with our Goldade ancestral family chart, to present the Reiss family ancestral chart in this book.

Pedigree

Chart #1

Chart of
Magdalena Reiss (9)

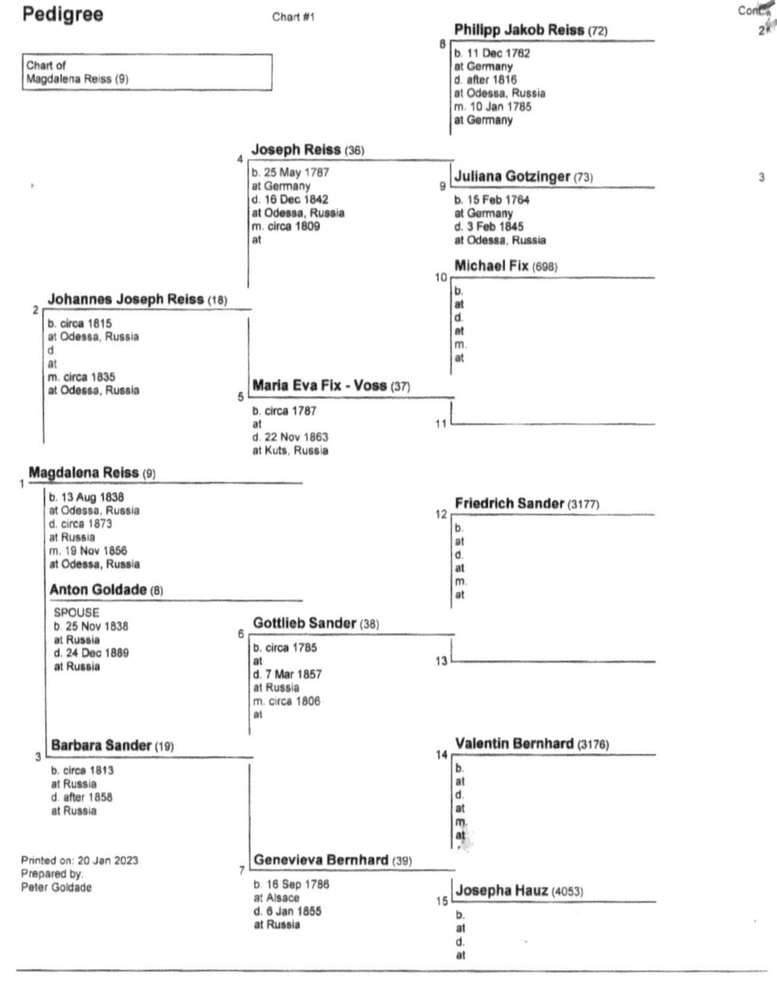

Printed on: 20 Jan 2023
Prepared by:
Peter Goldade

Cont. 2

3

Pedigree

Chart #2

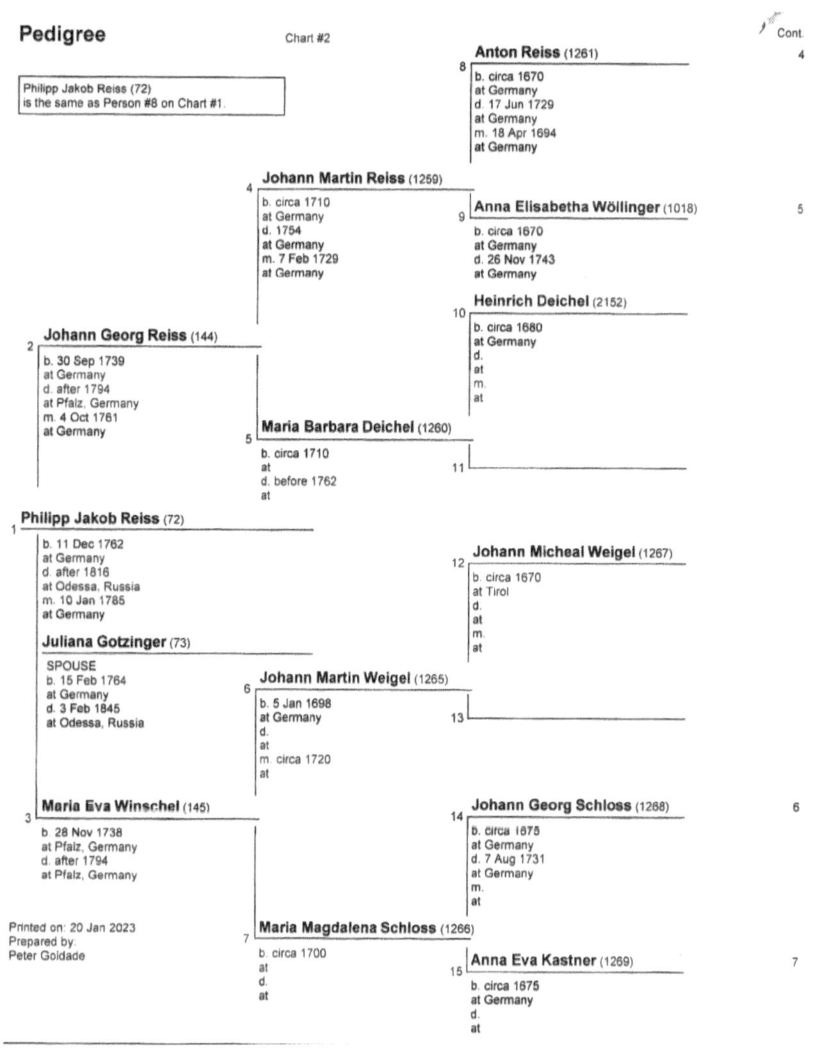

Pedigree

Chart #3

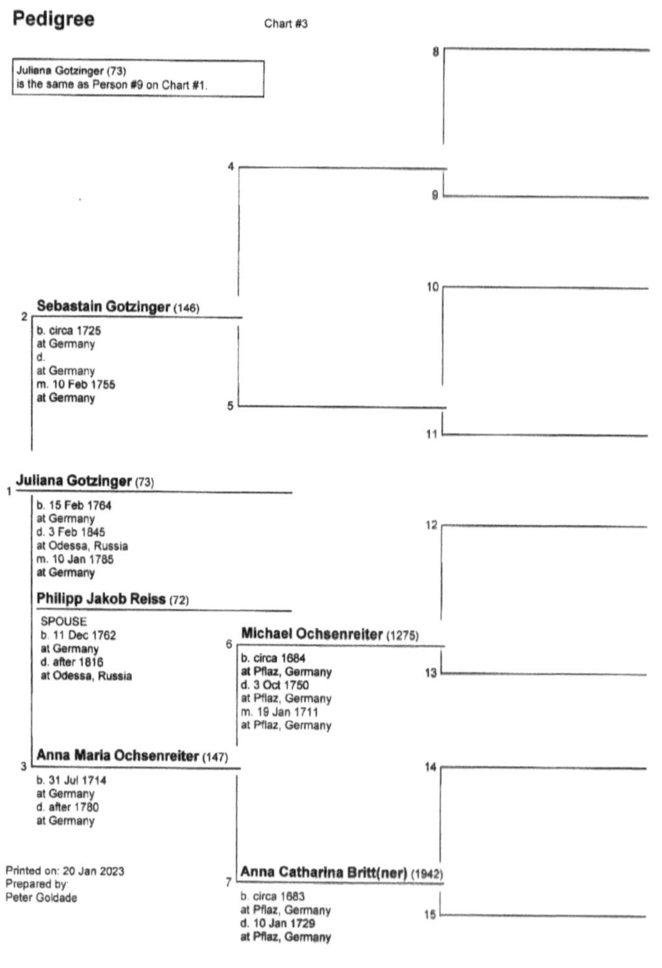

Printed on: 20 Jan 2023
Prepared by:
Peter Goldade

Pedigree

Chart #4

Anton Reiss (1261)
is the same as Person #8 on Chart #2.

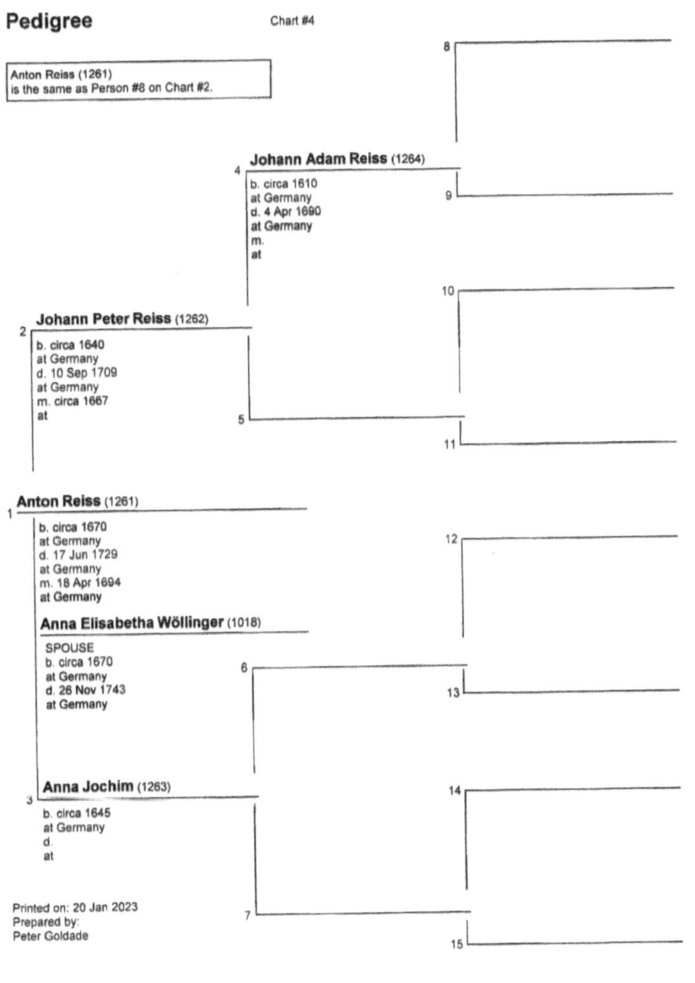

Printed on: 20 Jan 2023
Prepared by:
Peter Goldade

Pedigree

Chart #5

Anna Elisabetha Wöllinger (1018)
is the same as Person #9 on Chart #2.

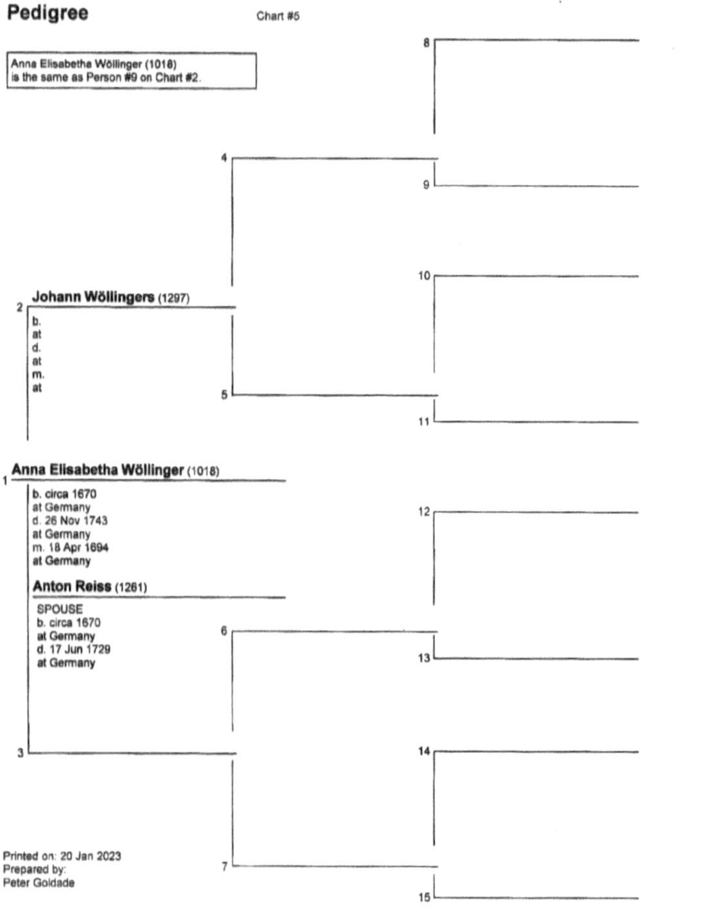

Printed on: 20 Jan 2023
Prepared by:
Peter Goldade

Pedigree

Chart #6

Johann Georg Schloss (1268)
is the same as Person #14 on Chart #2.

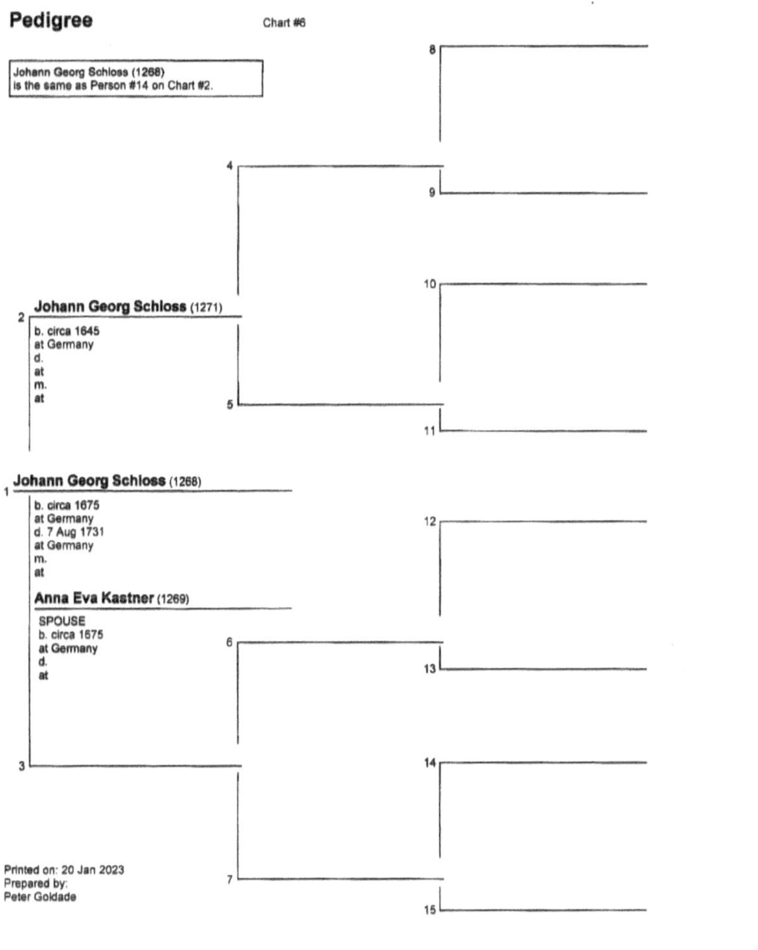

Printed on: 20 Jan 2023
Prepared by:
Peter Goldade

Pedigree

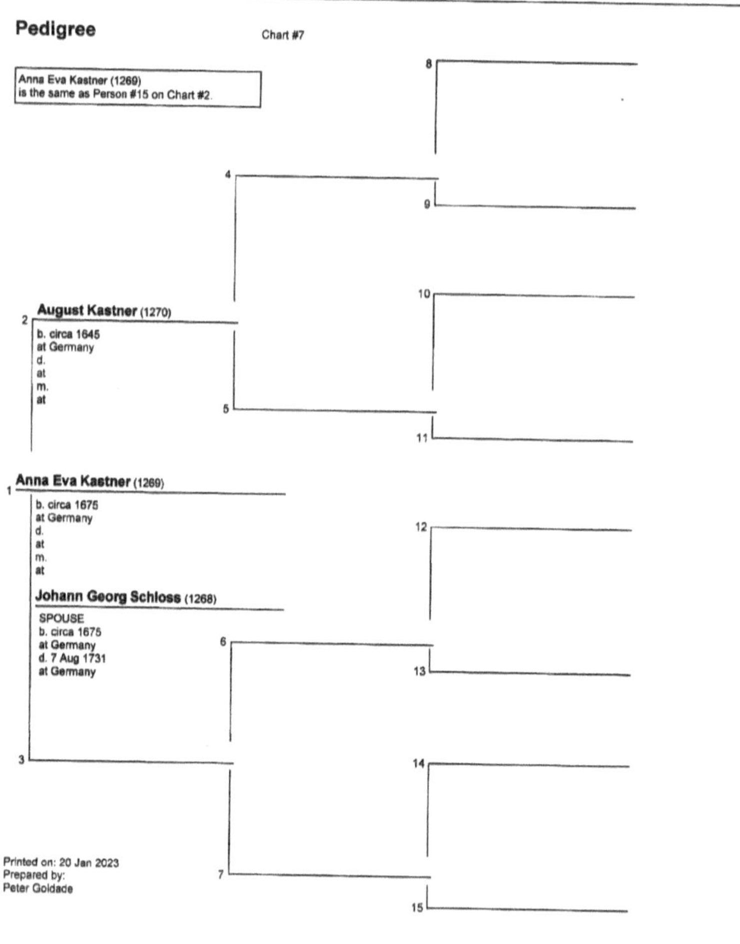

Printed on: 20 Jan 2023
Prepared by:
Peter Goldade

*"Those who deny freedom to others
deserve it not for themselves."*

Abraham Lincoln

Chapter 7

Johannes Goldade Family story

Along with the journey of my genealogy project, an equal quest was to determine the fate of all of my relatives who had stayed in Russia. One of my relatives who had stayed in Russia was Johannes Goldade. Johannes Goldade was born on 29 April 1900 in the Kutschurgan village of Selz. He was the son of Joseph Goldade and Maria Anna Wald. Johannes was my second cousin once removed.

On 25 November 1924 Johannes married Regina Eisenzimmer. Regina she was born on 11 February 1906 and was the daughter of Wilhelm Eisenzimmer and Marianne Eisenzimmer.

I have been retrieving Russian Repression and civil records from the Odessa State Archive, for over 20 years. Among these records were numerous files, relating to residents and their activity in the Kutschurgan villages. I have included these files in my book *Life under Tyranny*. Information regarding Johannes Goldade appears in a number of these files.

The files that include Johannes, provide some details in the early years of his life. File R8-1-94 Titled About registration and striking off the books Men liable for call-up born 1888-1921. Here Johannes is listed as "works for a Province Committee."

However, later file 58-1-32a Titled List of Military call-ups from the village of Selz, 3 September 1919. Here, Johannes is called up as a recruit. Johannes had to serve 3 years in the Russian military.

Another file, File R111-1-10 Titled Party Archives of the CPSU (Communist Party of the Soviet Union) Odessa Region Committee. Dated 20 September

1933. Sub titled Personal File of Goldade, Johannes son of Joseph. Worker at the Telmann state farm, station Jeremeyevka (aka Bischofsfeld), Selz district. Here Johannes is identified as having been a party candidate-member since 1932. However, it appears that Johannes had made amends, as he had been accused of having been in a category of 'sympathizers and politically ignorant.' Among other things the file goes on to state, that his:

Social origin - was poor

Social status – a state farm worker, a worker since 1913

education – elementary

Nationality – German

Public party load – medical aid

These three were the only files which I have retrieved, that specifically mentioned Johannes. Johannes was not identified in any other file as having been labelled a kulak or having a trade. Therefore, the only assumption that can be made is, that Johannes was a man of average means.

When the German army retreated from Russia in 1944, they evacuated most of the ethnic Germans who were living in Southern Russia. Selz, was the last village to evacuate. By the time that Selz evacuated, all of the bridges had been destroyed. In order to cross the Dniester River, the Selz villagers were forced to use a small ferry. Only about a third of the Selz villagers had crossed the Dniester River, before the Russians sunk the ferry.

Obviously, Johannes and his family had made a successful crossing, because the next information that we have for Johannes and his family is a EWZ record. When the ethnic Germans had evacuated the territories of Russia, they were resettled in German occupied areas, mostly in current Poland. While these ethnic Germans were in the German held areas, they were granted German naturalization. The people were processed through the 'Einwandererzentralstelle'. Known by the acronym EWZ. The translation of Einwandererzentralstelle is Immigration control Center. These records hold a wealth of family information.

Upon arriving in Poland, Johannes Goldade and his family were initially resettled in the village of Grenzhausen. The Polish name of the village is Stupca. It was only called Grenzhausen during the German occupation of the early 1940s. However, Johannes and his family were later moved to the town of Konin, where they received their German naturalization on 1 October 1944.

The EWZ record lists the family. We have the father Johannes and his wife Regina. Their children:

Son - Nikolaus born 11 March 1929.

Daughter - Theresia born 27 May 1934.

Son - Eugenius 25 April 1938.

Daughter - Maria born 8 July 1941.

Daughter - Elisabeth born 9 June 1944.

There is a sad notation in the EWZ record. It states that Regina had chicken pox at a young age. Due to the disease, she was completely blind in less than ten years. It is remarkable that even being blind, Regina was a Mother to 5 children.

Note: Joseph Height's book *Paradise on the Steppe* on page 264 has a 1944 plot map of the village Selz. The originators of the map have Eugenius as the head of the household. This is erroneous, as the head of the household was Johannes. Eugenius was only 6 years old in 1944.

In the mid-1990s I started my endeavor to locate my relatives in Europe. I had a good amount of success in finding relatives in Germany. However, there also was some disappointment in not being able to find all of the closer relatives. Included in the relatives that I was not able to find, were members of the Johannes Goldade family.

In addition to the normal methods of locating people, I also referred to the Russian 'Filtration Camp Records', which I had retrieved from the Odessa State Archive. After the war, the Russians were apprehending people who had fled from the Russian held territories. The apprehensions took place all across Europe. This included countries such as Germany, Poland, Austria, Romania, etc. In many cases the captured were held in Filtration Camps. The filtration camp records are a great asset for any research. The records state the family unit that was apprehended, and in many cases they also state the location of apprehension and the labor camp/resettlement camp to which they were send. The EWZ and the Filtration records are great companion records, for comparison of the family unit at different periods. The EWZ records list the family units, which consisted after the Trek to the German controlled areas and the Filtration records list the family unit at the time of the Russian apprehension after the war.

Unfortunately, in this case, no Filtration Camp Record was found for the Johannes Goldade family. This left a void for finding the family, all that I could hope for was that they were living some place in Russia or Kazakhstan. Additionally, since we do not have a filtration record, we do not know whether Johannes, while in Poland, had been conscripted into the German military or whether he was with the family when they were apprehended by the Russians.

In addition to referring to documents to locate the family, I also queried relatives living in Germany, Belarus and Russia. This was all to no avail, as no one had any communication with the family after they had left the village of Selz in 1944.

In the early 2000s an acquaintance went to Moscow to conduct some research. While doing her research, she came across a document regarding a Nikolaus Goldade and made a copy or me. This find was a god send for me, as we now know where the family had been send after their apprehension.

The document that the Lady found was from Ministry of Federation Affairs of the Russia Federation and stated that Nikolaus Goldade age 18 son of Johannes Goldade was at the Onegy labor camp.

The Onegy labor camp was close to the villages of Yarnema and Ulitino, which are in the Plesetsk district of the Arkhangelsk Oblast of Russia. The Arkhangelsk Oblast is in the northern most part of Russia and is roughly 600 miles (1,000 km) due north of Moscow.

The following is the title page of the document found by my acquaintance. It states that Nikolaus Goldade had attempted an escape, was captured and sentenced to 3 years of hard labor.

**"Ministry of Federation Affairs of National
and Migratory Politics of the Russian
Federation and the Public Academy of
Sciences Relating to the Russian Germans"**
The document is a

"Collection of Articles of Germans in Russia"

By **T. Saburova**

Published in

Moscow 2006

This article states that in May of 1947 Nicolaus Goldade age 18 the son of Johannes Goldade along with some other men attempted to escape from the Onegy re-settlement/labor camp. They were captured and sentenced to 3 years in a forced Labor/Gulag camp.

＋＋◆◆◆＋＋

This document provided information previously unknown, that Nikolaus Goldade had been send to the Onegy resettlement camp. The remainder of the family could also have been send to the Onegy camp, or settled on one of the neighboring villages of Yarnema or Ulitino after their apprehension. The only exception would be the father Johannes, if he had been conscripted into the German military and had not been reunited with the family. A filtration record, or a Russian resettlement passport document would have answered that question.

The question now is, why did Nikolaus attempt to escape? Was he frustrated for being incarcerated for only being an ethnic German? Or was he now the primary caregiver for his blind mother and younger siblings and wanted to get back to care for them? We will never know.

The fate of the Johannes family never left my mind and I would periodically devote some time to search for the Family. Around 2018 my dear friends in Germany, Sergey and Mila Koretnikov agreed to assist me. On one of his trips to Moscow, Sergey found the following book.

TRANSACTIONS
of Vologda Society for Studying North Lands

Issue XVIII

Materials of inter-regional schoolchildren's contest
on scientific study of local lore "Piece through culture"

Vologda 2011

In 2011 the Russian village of Yarnema was celebrating their school's jubilee. In conjunction with the celebration, they had a contest on the scientific study of local lore "Peace through Culture." The contest articles written by the high students from the village of Yarnema were than combined under "Transactions of Vologda Society for Studying North Lands."

The students selected various topics to enter the contest. In preparing for her project a student, Ludmila Mutovkina discovered that among the surnames of students who had attended the school, were those typical of ethnic Germans.

Ms. Mutovkina was intrigued with her discovery of the German surnames and decided to further her investigation and found that in the 1950s ethnic Germans had attended their school. The question of how and why Germans appeared in her village, led to her discovery that in the 1940s and 1950s there had been a German resettlement camp in the nearby village of Ulitino and a forced labor camp in the nearby village of Onege.

Based on this discovery, Ms. Mutovkina decided to base her submission for the contest on this subject. In addition to researching archived documents, Ms. Mutovkina also interviewed some of the older residents of the village of Yarnema, who remembered the time of the Germans living in the village. The result of the interviews revealed, that the displaced Germans from the resettlement camp had lived in harmony with the villagers of Yarnema. While the villagers had many fond memories of the German people, the one that probably had the best culinary touch was the one who remembered the great German bread baker.

Ms. Mutovkina wrote a spectacular article, she discloses the lives of the ethnic Germans who had lived in the resettlement camps and names many of the Germans who at one time had lived in her village. However, for myself Ms. Mutovkina provided another chapter for my relatives, the family of Johannes Goldade. In a matter of less than 5 years, the family of 7 had been reduced to 2. This was solely due to the inhuman treatment of the people who had been send to the resettlement camps. Ms. Mutovkina mentions that the mother Regina had died. The two small girls Maria and Elisabeth are not mentioned, so obviously they also had died. The father Johannes is not mentioned, thus we do not know what happened to him. Ms. Mutovkina states that the daughter Theresia wandered off into the woods not to be heard of again. Here we have several unanswered questions; what caused Theresia to wander into the forest, was she despondent, was she looking for food or was she looking for someone. What happened to Theresia, was she attacked by a human or animal predator, did she succumb to the elements or did she starve?

This is the last documentation that I have for the brothers Nikolaus and Eugenius Goldade, as with the rest of the family, I do not know what happened to them.

The story of my relative Johannes and his family is typical of what had happened to many ethic German families, who had been living in Russia at that time. Prior to the war, these people were enjoying their families in Russia. In 1941 many were forcibly evicted to Siberia, etc.

In 1944 others were evacuated to Poland and in 1945 many of these were apprehended and also forcibly send to Siberia, etc. During the resettlement process, the men and boys over the age of 16 were separated from their families and send to labor camps. Quite often there was further separation, as women also were compelled to heavy labor.

In summation, regarding the fate of the Johannes Goldade family... we can only make assumptions. The father is not mentioned in Ms. Mutovkina's article. Therefore, the most logical assumption is that he was conscripted into the German military and was a casualty of the war. Additionally, Johannes was not on any of the after the war MVD arrest lists, which I retrieved meaning that he had not been apprehended after the war or taken as a POW. The mother Regina being blind and not having an adult male available to provide care was doomed. While Theresia and Eugenius may have tried to forage for food, this may have been futile, as due to their geographical location of the Plesetsk region of long harsh winters and cold temperatures the opportunity for success would have been very limited. It is a well-known fact that the people who were placed in the labor and resettlement camps were not provided with adequate clothing, shelter or food. Therefore, Regina most likely starved or succumb to the elements. The two little girls Maria and Elisabeth, most likely met the same fate as their mother, again either starved or succumb to the elements. We are told that Theresia wandered off into the woods, not to be heard from or seen again. One can only use your imagination as to what happened to her. Ms. Mutovkina, tells us that Nikolaus and Eugenius were alive in 1955, but there is no further information regarding the two boys. It is only if Russia would be willing to release the records of that era, that we would know the fate of all of the people who were displaced during and after the war.

In the case of my relative Johannes and his family, they had been living in the Kutschurgan village of Selz, Russia. In 1944, they were evacuated to the village of Grenzhausen/Stupca, Poland and later moved to Konin, Poland. In 1945 they were apprehended by the Russians and taken to the Plesetsk District of the Archangelsk Oblast in the North of Russia.

In late 2022 and early 2023 Sergey Koretnikov became a detective and found the email address for Ms. Mutovkina. This was quite a feat, as Ms. Mutovkina was now married and had a new surname. Sergey was successful in contacting Ms. Mutovkina.

My utmost gratitude to Sergey and Mila Koretnikov for their assistance in finding this document and locating Ms. Mutovkina and to Ms. Mutovkina, for researching, writing the article and granting me the permission to reprint her great article.

The following is Ms. Mutovkina's complete article with her permission for me to reprint.

TRANSACTIONS
of Vologda Society for Studying North Lands

Issue XVIII

Materials of inter-regional schoolchildren's contest
on scientific study of local lore "Piece through culture"

Vologda 2011

Pages 37-45

Ludmila Mutovkina,
*11th-form student of "Yarnema general education
high school" (Plesetsk District, Archangelsk region)*

REPATRIATED GERMANS IN ULITINO
(PLESETSK DISTRICT, ARCHANGELSK REGION)
IN 1930's-1950's

Preparing for the jubilee of the Yarnema School and reviewing archival documents, we noticed that lists of students who studied in our school in 1950s included many German names. Thus, for example 20 names were put on the second-form list in 1955 and 7 of them were Germans; Dillmann, Klementine - Hunkel, Hilda - Dick, Selma - William, Margaretha - Seiler, Irma - Rosenbach, Adelaide and Scholl, Willi. In the 1957-1958 lists we came across just one German last name – Wahler. We then grew interested in knowing from where these Germans came, when they came, when and why they left.

Russian Germans are a part of the population of our country, they have lived the whole history with Russia's other peoples to have been and remain Russians. Foreigners came to Russia as far back as under Peter the First, but their inflow especially intensified during the reign of Catherine the Second who invited Germans to develop virgin lands of Volga and other South Russia regions.

During the soviets (in 1924) the ASSR [*Autonomous Soviet Socialist Republic*] of Volga Germans was founded with its centre in the town of Engels,

German colonies in South Ukraine were retained as well. Germans lived with Russians in harmony. The events of WWI and the Revolution deteriorated the relations. The beginning of forced resettlement of Germans from the regions they had developed to the North of Europe was bound up with the collectivization which started in 1929 when prosperous villagers, so called "kulaks" and "kulak's henchmen" were deprived of their property, land, cattle, houses and sent to uninhabited regions of the country including the North. In that way, the fates of Russian and German villagers were equally tragic during the collectivization.

Another mass of specially resettled Germans has appeared in the North during the Great Patriotic war in August of 1941. The ASSR of Volga Germans was liquidated with hundreds of thousands Germans sent to Siberia, Kazakhstan, Middle Asia and the North as "socially dangerous". The reason for resettlement was officially specified in the USSR Supreme Soviet Presidium's Edict of 28 August 1941 – available reliable information about "thousands and tens of thousands of spies and wreckers living in the ASSR who, by the signal given from Germany were instructed to make explosions in districts populated by Volga Germans". In order to avoid "substantial bloodshed", the resettlement program was carried out.

Although there were many patriots of Russia among the German population, Germans were not called up to fight at the front. In March 1942 all German men aged 15 - 55 and women of 16 - 50, except for those pregnant and having children under 3 years of age were mobilized to a Labour Army where they were treated as betrayers and kept in camps enclosed with barbed wire, etc., and guard. Labour service people built roads, factories, bridges. Khariukov, S. K. writes that his father was sent along with his two brothers to build a railway bridge across the river of North-Dvina for getting to the town of Kotlas. The NKVD camp where they were kept accommodated over 10,000 people, mainly Volga Germans. One can conclude that by drudgery, that these people made their contribution to a victory over fascism as well.

Not less of a tragic fate happened to Germans in the South of the country who got under the occupation due to fast advance of German troops. Although in September 1941 the State committee for defense made a decision for the resettling of ethnic Germans from the front-line area, only 5 - 15% of those were resettled. During the period of 1941 - 1943 Germans living in Zhitomir, Nikolayev, Odessa, Dnepropetrovsk, Zaporozhye and other regions dwelling in the territory occupied by German and Romanian troops. If they got a German registration they received foodstuffs and enjoyed some other privileges from the occupiers.

When the Red army began its offensive in this direction in the fall of 1943, many "Russian" Germans were sent by fascists to the West, to Poland and Germany where manpower was then needed. It is hard to say how many had moved on their free will and how many moved under constraint. A part of them received German citizenship, especially if someone from the family had joined up in the German army. The 1943 - 1944 evacuation from native villages together with retreating German troops was also forced because people were afraid of repressions from the soviets for "going over to the enemy" but there, in Germany they were not received friendly either. According to E. A. Dmitrieva German women recollected that they were treated with hostility and contempt and were called "Black-Sea swine".

When the war ended, tens of thousands of Germans from the USSR gathered in the Soviet zone in Germany. Most of them were repatriated in 1945 - 1946.

It is said in G. Walter's article "Зона полного покоя" [*The Zone of Absolute Peace*] that from 150,000 Germans found themselves in the West of Germany, another half of that number was also delivered by the allies to the USSR. Thus, about 280,000 Germans were sent back to the Homeland. The Soviet authorities promised to return them to the places of their former living, but some of them were arrested and sent to correctional labour camps for the betrayal of the Homeland, with the rest, mostly women and children, forwarded to special settlements to be under surveillance of Commandant's offices and disenfranchised for a long period of time. The USSR Supreme Soviet Presidium's Edict of 26 November 1948 condemned children and grandchildren of people of German nationality to everlasting living at the places of their parents' exile.

According to the MVD Archangelsk regional department information cited in T. Saburova's article "Ethnic Germans in the North" by 1 July 1947 there were 3,638 German families (11,392 people) specially resettled in the Archangelsk region. T. Saburova notes that most of them were repatriated, with the rest resettled from the autonomous republic. It is also said there that German repatriates built the Archangelsk paper group of enterprises, Onega hydrolytic works, Kodino pulp and paper mill, works in Onega and

Plesetsk districts. Germans from Crimea, Odessa, Saratov, Dnepropetrovsk and Zhitomir regions lived in Onega, a special settlement for timber mills №.'s 32 and 33. Repatriates from Zaporozhye, Ropstov-on-Don, Stalino and Kiev regions dwelled in Kodino. There were 26 special settlements in Plesetsk district where dekulakized, deported and repatriated Germans did as well as labour servicers, among these settlements – Lomovoye, Wimuga, Emtsa, Obozerskaya, Plesetsk tractor station, Plesetsk works №. 1, Beloye Ozero, Lelma, Kasskoye, Kochmas, Karasowo, Kostyly, Kurgan, Perekop, Malinovka, Vodopad, Izhoshka, Glubokovsky, Volchanitsa, Shypechnoye and Lipakowo. This demonstrates that specially resettled Germans' manpower was used when building all works in Archangelsk region.

At the narrow-gauge railway building.

The beginning of the settlement of Ulitino is closely connected with these events. When the Paberezh state timber industry enterprise (the one located in our settlement was then called by this name) started to work, its office was situated in the village of Yarnema where many workers lodged with local inhabitants. The building of our settlement was started somewhat later, in 1947 - 1948 and a narrow-gauge railway (NGR) was needed for the transportation of timber. Specially resettled German repatriates were brought here to build the railway. The day of 12 October 1949 is fixed in the house-registers of Yarnema village soviet, as the date of arrival for most of them, but it is also possible that information about Germans who came earlier has just been lost. E. A. Borodina who already worked in Yarnema in 1948 specifies that this is the year for the date of their arrival. We have found in various sources of 77 German surnames and information about 160 specific persons not counting children under school age and those we questioned. E. A. Dmitrieva states that a total of 150 families had then been sent there. Birth years for 103 people are specified in the house-registers mentioned, so we were able to determine their ages. Only 34 persons were of age by the war's beginning, including 11 males and among them were the 3; Bauer, Carl (1913), Hust, Wilhelm (1911) and Scholl, Heinrich (1914) they were brought from the places of imprisonment to Ulitino to join their families. A total of eight people came from ITL [*Correctional Labour Camps*] back to the settlement of Ulitino in the 1950's.

Building of new houses in Ulitino in the 1950's.

Information obtained from the house-registers has made it possible to ascertain that their birth places were from the villages of Dnepropetrovsk, Zhitomir, Zaporozhye, Nikolayev and Odessa regions. Many of these villages apparently were places of compact living of Russian Germans because following German appellatives can be found there – Peterstal, Eugenfeld, Lenintal, Katharinental, Furstenwerden, Sparrau, Mariental, Johannestal,

Kassel, Rosenfeld, etc. All of these villages were situated in the area of the South regions of Ukraine (the Dnepr river right bank) were occupied by fascists during first months of the war. According to E. A. Dmitrieva who worked with a team on the railway construction along with Germans, they were sent to Germany in November 1944 to be then repatriated i.e. brought from there back to the USSR, not to their native villages but to special settlements to be under surveillance of the commandant's offices. They didn't like to tell about their trying experience but sometimes told those whom they trusted. It is not yet possible to verify their recollections since we were not able to find information in the documents available regarding their past, nor did we succeed in contacting those whose names we were able to find.

E. A. Borodina recounted that German families were brought from Onega to Gorodok which is 10 km away of Ulitino, by barges to further be transported to Ulitino by tractors along the river bank. It is unknown how they settled down at a new place, but what is known is that at the beginning of 1950's they lived in 4 barracks (hostels) situated at the Stakhanov and Lesnaya Streets. Machine-road-building team № 2 of Yarnema building column became their place of work and the railway building Yarnema station was their residence, this was the way our settlement Ulitino was then called. Instead of passports they had references issued by the MVD Plesetsk district department in October 1949.

According to E. A. Dmitrieva Germans also lived in settlement Pivka (a part of the town of Onega), perhaps they worked in Onega and built factories. E. A. Dmitrieva tells about Germans' life and work this way: "I came to the settlement in 1952 to work at the narrow-gauge railway construction within a team along with Germans who started it. By 1952 a locomotive depot had been built as well as a car shop for repairs of open goods trucks, storehouse and a water-tower for locomotives. In 1953, Germans worked at the settlement of Pyssoma construction as well, to be away during a whole week and at home just one day off. It was hard work to fell trees, hack knots, make embankment, put ties and rails down. Everybody was under surveillance of commandant Spyrov. Every morning and every evening the one responsible for a group consisting of several families had to make a report to him that no one had escaped. He was brutal to be afraid of, one woman said she was very ill (had a stomach cramp) every time he passed by her windows. The rules set for Germans were severe — one could not go farther than the village of Ragoziny, going across the river was allowed for the one having a permit only although the village soviet was situated over the river, 2 meters dropping in the river meant escape. German women told that Spyrov summoned Netz who was just 15 years old to his office, set a gun against her head and demanded to say where her father was. She and her mother really did not know where. Ketterling, Elizabetha's mother recalled that Losing's son was arrested in the town because he was walking to another factory by his job for a spare part without a written permit so was sentenced to 8-year imprisonment to serve that in a camp in Dzhezkazgan".

18-year-old Nicolaus Goldade is mentioned in T. Saburova's article, he who in May 1947 escaped from special settlement Onega, was captured and for that was sentenced to 3 years of ITL. According to the house-register Theresia Goldade and her brother whose first name is unknown ** did work in Ulitino where on 22 January 1950 their brother Nicolaus came back from an ITL. Since all the information fits, we think that he is that very person mentioned in T. Saburova's article.

All those questioned by us remember Germans as diligent, serious, skillful and honest people. Plots of land beyond the settlement were allotted to them to plant potatoes they enclosed the field with joint fences and together went out to repair it when needed. They were people from villages who had not lost their farming skills, so they also had chickens, goats, pigs. There always were people on duty in the barracks; who scrubbed the floors, whitewashed the walls, the area around their houses always was very clean, it was without any kind of rubbish.

E. A. Dmitrieva, as many others, can recollect Markus Huber who worked at a bakery and cooked buns and even cakes on high days and holidays: "He made a bread, one had never even dreamt of!" "They were on very friendly terms with each other their children grew up diligent from the earliest childhood. They brought water on yokes from the river with buckets touching the ground!" – E. A. Dmitrieva narrates. V. S. Mukovozchik recalls German kids studied well. V. V. Kiselev still remembers these people to be pretty clean and very decent. Despite very dirty streets it was strange for local boys to see "the always clean foot-bridges by houses where the Germans lived, they left their shoes on the porch, the windows were curtained and various flowers were planted by the house". He is even now surprised that in those hungry years and in their circumstances they still took care of the beauty of their houses.

All the mentioned recollect that Germans worked hard, but on Sundays they were well-dressed and tried to take a rest, they did have such a custom. K. M. Dautova says: "They would rather do all of the house work on Saturday and work until late into the night! They did not like to drink wine, nor did they behave like hooligans, but lived in harmony concerning everything".

Everybody questioned only said good things regarding Germans' relations with local inhabitants. V. S. Mukovozchik said that locals treated them kindly, so did the Germans. V. V. Kiselev who was a schoolboy then recollected that they, having lost their fathers during the war often beat German boys bearing hated names "Adolf", "Fritz" but their mothers reproached them with saying that children are not guilty of anything.

E. A. Dmitrieva – «Germans were very thrifty, they did not go to a dining-hall because it was too expensive for them, so they took food from home a round of rye-bread spread with thin layer of butter to just cover holes and added milk to a bottle to whiten tea – here is a lunch. But when Maria Leer saw me having nothing to eat but just cowberries picked in the forest (I had no money when I arrived here) she shared potatoes and onion taken from her home for lunch with me. In the evening Ketterlings gave me some potatoes they had already grown in 1952, to supply me with something to cook for myself and my daughter. They had probably been half starved themselves so felt pity for others. When I hurt my leg, Mehlhaf, Cecilia treated it, although being afraid of commandant Spirov who punished her for "quackery", the leg eventually recovered from that wound. Elizabetha Ketterling's mother had a sewing-machine of her own and using it, she earned her living. Young Germans were on good terms with Russians, some lads even were friends with Russian girls. Thus, for example Faina from Belorussia was a friend to Karl Langolf, commandant Spirov told her: "You have just two options – either friendship with Germans or remaining in the Komsomol, make your choice". She subsequently left him and Carl married a German girl. I was on friendly terms with Ketterling, Lydia and her mother, I went across the river to register Lydia's son at the village soviet when he was born in October 1954, even to be named Vladimir by me as his godmother. Germans did not say much about what they had to go through. They did not express any resentment against the government and Russians, in general they rarely complained. Just once Catharina Kary told me: "Shenia, Shenia (the elderly people speak Russian worse than the young ones, they do not articulate the letter "ж" [ʒ]) … we are "fritzes", "fascists" but you, what are you suffering for? Our day will come!"».

It follows from that said above that the simple inhabitants of our settlement did not feel hatred towards Germans. Despite that they spoke another language among themselves, having different habits, had not become quite "ours" after 6 years of living in the settlement Germans have left fond memories behind. E. A. Dmitrieva said with bitterness: "If they had not left, would our settlement be such as it is now!"

After a prominent visit to the USSR by the Federal Chancellor of Germany, Konrad Adenauer in September 1955, the commandant's office was abolished specially resettled Germans received passports and were allowed to leave the place of banishment. However, the ban imposed on their return to native lands still remained valid. "The building column of the No. 2 machine-road-building team" discontinued its existence in 1956 (at that time it was headed by Undozerov) and the workers were transferred to the Paberezh state timber industry enterprise. All of the Germans left the settlement during the period from the end of 1955 – to the beginning of 1956. E. A. Dmitrieva – "I saw Dollinger's reference stating that they had the right to reside all over the USSR except for the place from where they had lived before the evacuation to Germany. Nevertheless, it was said that some of them did travel to their homeland, saw that their houses had not been destroyed during the war, but were immediately sent away from there and not allowed to live in their native house". From the school book of directions where pupils' departures are fixed, we got to know that many Germans left for Alma-Ata, Akmolinsk region, Kryvoy-Rog, Leninakan, Stalinabad, Sverdlovsk and other towns of the USSR, some of them departed to Onega. Nothing is yet known about their further fate.

Some of them probably recollected their living in Ulitino because they corresponded with local inhabitants. Amalie Losing who left for Kirgisia in 1955 wrote letters to E. A. Dmitrieva, N. M. Diadkyn was in correspondence with some German as well. Klassen, Erna wrote to T. A. Klykova and visited here after 1976. As E. A. Dmitrieva remembers, Welter, Immanuel came here to get references regarding his work in 1940's – 1950's (later on he immigrated to Germany).

List of Germans who resided in Ulitino in the 1940's – 1950's

Ord. №	Name	Birth year	Birth place	Additional information
1.	Eichele, Elsa dau of Johann			12 Dec. 1949 gave birth to son
2.	Babenko, Julia dau of Jacob	1914	Sazonovka, Odessa	12 Oct. 1949 – 14 Nov. 1955, two children
3. 4.	Bauer, Carl son of Carl Bauer, Bertha dau of Christian	1913 1917	Peterstal, Odessa	29 Apr. 1953 returned from ITL12. 12 Oct. 1949 – 14 Nov. 1955, two children
5. 6.	Bender, Clara dau of Peter Bender, Amalie	1928	Iraklievka, Odessa	12 Oct. 1949 – 14 Nov. 1955
7.	Bodamer, Melitha dau of Robert	1921		12 Aug. 1950 marriage application with Neigel, Georg son of C. (born in 1922)
8. 9.	Brandt, Johann son of Leopold Brandt, Amalie dau of Peter	1932 1933	Krasnorechka, Zhit. Iraklievka, Odessa	12 Oct. 1949 - 14 Nov. 1955 12 Oct. 1949 - 14 Nov. 1955
10.	Brom, Selma dau of Albert	1935	Natalie, Zhitomir	12 Oct.1949 – 14 Nov. 1955

11. 12.	Buss, Ernst son of Friedrich Buss, Erna dau of Ernst	1894 1923	Uvarovka, Zhitomir	12 Oct. 1949 – 14 Nov. 1955, Both worked at the NGR
13. 14.	Wahler, Joseph Joseph's mother			Lived in the settlement until the end of the 1970's
15. 16.	Weber, Wilhard son of Balthasar Weber, Eduard son of Jacob	1929 1929	Eugenfeld, Zaporozhye	12 Oct. 1949 – 14 Nov. 1955 dates for both W & E. Marriage application (with Lukanovskaya, L. P.)
17.	Weller			
18. 19. 20.	Welter, Imanuel son of Johann Welter, Barbara dau of Johann Welter, Martha dau of Emil (Imanuel's wife)	1926 1927 1927	Dobry Lug, Odessa Dobry Lug, Odessa Alexandropol, Dnepropetrovsk	12 Oct. 1949 – 14 Nov. 1955, came to Ulitino for documents, later left for Germany Arrived 12 Dec. 1949, 19 Nov. 1949 gave birth to son
21.	Wetstein, Reinhard son of Martin	1930	Lenintal, Dnepropetrovsk	12 Oct. 1949 – 14 Nov. 1955
22. 23.	Willms, Catharina dau of David Willms, Margaretha	1912	Furstenwerden, Zaporozhye	12 Oct. 1949 – 14 Nov. 1955 1955 went to school, 30 Jan. 1956 left for Sverdlovsk
24. 25.	Wink, Gerta dau of Emil Wink, Rosalia	1919	Chervonoarmeisky district, Zhitomir	12 Jan. 1956 departed from 6th form to Onega
26.	Gaaf, Immanuel son of Johann	1923	Katharinental, Nikol.	12 Oct.1949 - 14.Nov.1955

27.	Gaaf, Henrietta dau of Hieronimus	1927	Katharinental, Nikol.	12 Oct.1949 – 14 Nov. 1955, worked at a power-saw bench
28.	Harsch (two families)			
29.	Happeld, Alwin son of Albert	1929	Gorschyk, Zhitomir	12 Oct. 1949 - 14.Nov.1955
30.	Hafner, Johann son of Valentin			Married to Yury Savchenko's sister (left for Kazakhstan)
31. 32.	Hafner, Lydia dau of Valentin Hafner,Michael son of Valentin	1945 1948		1952 went to school 1956 went to school 05 June 1957 both departed to the Kustanai region
33. 34. 35. 36. 37.	Hupfner, Maria dau of Joseph Hupfner, Adelina dau of Joseph Hupfner, Eugenia dau of Jos. Hupfner, Vera dau of Joseph Hupfner, Pius son of Joseph	1923 1928 1930 1933	Stepanovka, Odessa Shevchenko, Odessa Shevchenko, Odessa Shevchenko, Odessa Shevchenko, Odessa	12 Oct. 1949 - 14 Nov.1955 all Married to Rieger
38. 39. 40.	Goldade, Nicolaus son of Johann Goldade, Theresia dau of Johann Goldade, (brother) **	1929	Selz, Odessa	22 Jan. 1950 Nicolaus arrived from ITL, no father, mother died, Theresia has been lost in the Pysoma forest.
41. 42.	Gretz,Philipp son of Michael Gretz, Eduard son of Michael	1931 1934	Novodvorovka, Zaporozhye	12 Oct. 1949 – 14 Nov. 1955 12 Oct. 1949 – 14 Nov. 1955
43.	Gross			

44. 45.	Huber, Markus son of Joseph			came to relatives after imprisonment, a baker
46. 47.	Huber, Christina dau of Joseph Huber, Agnesia dau of Joseph Huber, Regina dau of Joseph	1913 1926	Poniatovka, Odessa	12 Oct. 1949 - 14 Nov. 1955,
48. 49.	Hust, Wilhelm son of Jacob Hust, Rosina dau of Wilhelm	1911 1915	Iraklievka, Odessa	3 Feb. 1951 arrived to wife (?) 12 Oct. 1949 – 14 Nov. 1955
50. 51. 52.	Derzapf, Catharina dau of Martin Derzapf, Michael son of Martin Derzapf, Martin son of Martin	1928 1930 1935	Neu-Selz, Odessa	12 Oct. 1949 – 14 Nov. 1955
53. 54.	Dick, Maria dau of Peter Dick, Selma	1912	Sparau, Zaporozhye	12 Oct. 1949 – 14 Nov. 1955 Went to 5th form in 1955, 20 Feb. 1956 departed to Akmolinsk
55. 56. 57.	Dillman, Barbara dau of Georg Dillman, Clementine Dillman, Elizabetha	1920	Mariental, Odessa	12 Oct. 1949 – 14 Nov. 1955 Went to 5th form in 1955, left 5th form 12 Jan. 1956 left 6th form for Akmoilinsk

58.	Dollinger, Theodor son of Theodor	1910	Voinichewo, Odessa	12 Oct. 1949 – 14 Nov. 1955
59.	Dollinger,Walter son of Jacob (Theodor's nephew)	1931	Satowo, Sverdlovsk	Married a Ukrainian woman
60.	Dollinger, Erna			Timber examiner
--	Dollinger, Nelli			29 Feb. 1956 left 6th form for Krivy-Rog
61.	Efimchuk (married a German woman)			
62.	Seidel, (mother)			12 Oct. 1949 – 14 Nov. 1955
63.	Seidel, Ewald son of Emil	1928		
64.			Olgovka, Zaporozhye	
65.	Seidel, Zinaida			
66.	Seidel, Gerta			22 Feb. 1956 left 7th form for Leninakan
	Seidel, Gerhard			
67.	Seiler, Alfred son of Heinrich	1910	Johannestal, Odessa	12 Oct. 1949 – 14 Nov. 1955
68.		1912	Satowo, Odessa	
69.	Seiler, Paulina dau of Emil			Went to 5th form in 1955, 29 Jan. 1956 left for Krivy - Rog
	Seiler, Irma			
70.	Kazakovsky, Martin son of Martin	1926	Novodvorovka, Zaporozhye	20 Feb. 1953 arrived from Krasnoyarsk region
71.	Kazakovsky, Alwine dau of Andreas	1929	Cybuliovka/Neu-Gluckstal, Odessa	12 Oct. 1949 - 14.Nov. 1955
72.	Kary, Catharina (mother)			
73.		1929		
74.	Kary, Yury son of Anton	1931	Landau, Nikolayev	12 Oct. 1949 – 14 Nov. 1955 all
	Kary, Maria dau of Anton			

75.	Kessler, Rosina dau of Wilhelm	1934	khutor Vesely, Odessa	12 Oct. 1949 - 14.Nov. 1955, married Yury Kary
76.	Ketterling, Lydia dau of August	1925	Kassel, Odessa	12 Oct. 1949 – 14 Nov. 1955, in October 1954 gave birth to son Ketterling, Vladimir son of August
77.	Lydia's mother Paulina			
78.	Klassen, Erna and her 3 dau's			Came to Ulitino in late 1970's (?)
79.	Klassen, Lilia (daughter)			Left 7th form in 1956
80.	Keller, Catharina dau of Peter	1914	Odessa region	12 Oct. 1949 – 14 Nov. 1955
81. 82.	Kunkel, Augusta d. of Michael	1910 1937	Korostyshewo, Zhitomir	12 Oct. 1949 – 14 Nov. 1955
83.	Kunkel, Arthur son of Eduard Kunkel, Hilda			12 Oct. 1949 – 14 Nov. 1955 Went to 5th form in 1955, 26 Apr. 1956 left for Pavlodar
84.	Kurz, Gustav son of Christian (married a Ukrainian woman)	1902	Olkhovka, Zhitomir	12 Oct. 1949 – 14 Nov. 1955, worked as a water-carrier, buried at a German cemetery in Ulitiono
85.	Kuholik and his wife (Netz's parents)			

86.	Langolf, Carl son of Carl (and his brother)	1930	Rosenfeld, Slavgorod, Omsk	12 Oct. 1949 – 14 Nov. 1955 (27 Oct. 1950 marriage application with Huber, Regina dau Joseph)
87. 88.	Langolf, Melitha dau of Christoph (brother's wife) Langolf, Irene dau of Adolf	1931 1935	Kassel, Odessa Turchinka, Zhitomir	12 Oct. 1949 – 14 Nov. 1955
89. 90.	Leder, Almira dau of Ewald (Almira's mother)	1932	Yazovets, Zhitomir	12 Oct. 1949 – 14 Nov. 1955, worked at the NGR building
91.	Leer, Maria			Worked at the NGR building, left for Kazakhstan
92. 93.	Litau, Eugenie Eugenie's mother			16 Mar. 1956 left 5th form for Stalinabad (worked in a dining hall)
94.	Losing, Amalie dau of Andreas plus (other family members)	1921	Cybuliovka/Neu-Gluckstal, Odessa	12 Oct. 1949 – 14 Nov. 1955, left for Kirgizia

95.	Lukanovsky, (mother)	1934		Could treat people
96.	Lukanovsky, Linhard son of Michael	1937		12 Oct. 1949 – 14 Nov. 1955 for all
97.	Lukanovsky, Michael son of Michael	1929	Novodvorovka, Zaporozhye	
98.	Lukanovsky, Andreas son of Peter	1934		
99.	Lukanovsky, Joseph son of Peter	1927		Marriage application (with Weber, Eduard son of Jacob)
100.	Lukanovsky, Lucia d. of Peter			
101.	Lutz, Irene dau of Eduard	1945		Went to school in 1953, 8 Mar. 1957 left for Novosibirsk
102.	Lutz, Lilia		Odessa region	Left 5th form for Akmolinsk
103.	Lutz, Alwine dau of Johann Markovich … dau of Franz (sister to Slivka, Maria)			28 June 1950 gave birth to daughter
104.	Mehlhaf, Cecilia			Could treat people
105.	Mehlhaf, Emma			4 Nov. 1949 gave birth to dau.
106.	Mehlhaf, Melitha			
107.	Mehlhaf, Leopold			2 Mar. 1956 left 6th form for Onega
108.	Neigel, Georg son of Camilius	1927	Josephstal, Odessa	12 Oct. 1949 – 14 Nov. 1955, 12 Aug. 1950 marriage application (with Bodamer, Melitha)

109. 110.	Neufeld Johann s. of Abraham Neufeld Alma dau of Emil	1935 1935	Sparau, Zaporozhye Gorlovka, Zaporozh.	12 Oct. 1949 – 14 Nov. 1955 Married Seidel
111. 112.	Netz Lydia dau of Gustav Netz Irene	1919 1935?	Tomashevka, Zhitomir	12 Oct. 1949 – 14 Nov. 1955
113.	Obenauer Johann son of Reinhold Obenauer Helene dau of David	1921 1925	Vysokoye, Zaporozhye	October 20 arrived from ITL Residing since 1948, got a passport
114. 115. 116. 117. 118.	Pfeiffer, (mother) Pfeiffer, Joseph Pfeiffer, Catharina dau of Jos. Pfeiffer, Francisca Pfeiffer, Emma	1935	Razdelnaya district, Odessa region	5 daughters, husband came from ITL (a carpenter) 12 Oct. 1949 – 14 Nov. 1955 23 May 1956 left 6th form for Onega
119. 120.	Rieger, Michael s. of Wendelin Rieger Ludwig son of Michael	1904 1931	Kandel, Odessa	12 Oct. 1949 – 14 Nov. 1955 For all
121. 122.	Rosenbach, Ferdinand son of Ludwig Rosenbach, Adelaide	1908	Stolpetsk, Zhitomir	12 Oct. 1949 – 14 Nov. 1955 1955 went to 5th form, 13 Feb. 1956 left for Molotov
123. 124.	Rombs, Joseph Joseph's mother			1956 left 6th form for Onega

125. 126. 127.	Sautter, Irma dau of Heinrich Sautter, Lilia dau of Karl Sautter, Willi son of Karl	1908 1930 1934	Konoplewo, Odessa	12 Oct. 1949 – 14 Nov. 1955 For all
128.	Sidorenko			
129.	Sieter, Catharina dau of Franz	1931	Trikrynitsa, Zapor.	12 Oct. 1949 - 14. Nov. 1955
130.	Slivka, Maria dau of Franz (surname by marriage)	1935	Trikrynitsa, Zapor.	Married Ukrainian man in Ulitino, 10 Oct. 1956 left for Hust, Trans-Carpathian region
131. 132. 133.	Felske, Heinrich son of Eduard Felske, Erna dau of Emil Felske, Herbert son of Eduard	1919 1919	Martynovka, Zhitomir	Carpenter Ballaster Fell in love with Schwarz, Alma, threw himself under a locomotive, buried in Ulitino
134. 135. 136.	Fritz, Hilda dau of Michael (had a son) Fritz, Heinrich son of Edgar Fritz, Frieda dau of Abraham	1930 1934 1935	Janovka, Zhitomir Cecilivka, Zhitomir Sparau, Zaporozhye	12 Oct. 1949 – 14 Nov. 1955 for all
137. 138. 139.	Zeiter, Emil son of Wilhelm Zeiter, Emil son of Emil Zeiter, Martha dau of Leopold	1907 1931	Alexandropol, Dnepr Lenintal, Dnepr Krasnorechka, Zhit.	12 Oct. 1949 – 14 Nov. 1955 for all
140. 141.	Schatz, Elina Schatz, Rosa dau of Ferdinand	 1945		30. Apr. 1950 gave birth to daughter 8 Mar. 1957 left for Karaganda

No.	Name	Year	Place of origin	Notes
142. 143.	Schwarz, Ewald son of Albin Schwarz, Alma dau of Albin	1927 1933	Dubowo, Zhitomir	12 Oct. 1949 – 14 Nov. 1955 for all
144. 145.	Schilling, Hilda dau of August Schilling, Emil son of Emil	1912 1935	Alexandropol, Dnepropetrovsk	12 Oct. 1949 – 14 Nov. 1955 for all
146. 147.	Schmalz, Elizabetha dau of Thomas (and her father) Schmalz, Philomena dau of Thomas	1933 1943	Kandel, Odessa	12 Oct. 1949 – 14 Nov. 1955 8 Mar. 1957 left for Leninabad
148. 149. 150. 151.	Scholl, Heinrich son of Friedrich Scholl, Bertha dau of Peter Scholl, Elizabetha dau of Heinrich Scholl, Willi	1914 1904 1915	Irakliyevka, Odessa	16. July 1953 arrived from ITL, all lived in Belova's house at Lesnaya St., had 2 children 12 Oct. 1949 – 14 Nov. 1955 Went to 5th form in 1955
152.	Steinbach, Hugo son of Robert	1930	Krasnorechka, Zhitomir	12 Oct. 1949 – 14 Nov. 1955, head of a team of carpenters
153.	Stabler			Returned from ITL
154. 155.	Stock, Willi son of Wilhelm Stock, Linda dau of Wilhelm	1943 1945		Both left on 8 Mar. 1957

156.	Jungkind, Sivester son of Leopold,	1930	Novodvorovka, Zaporozhye Marienfeld, Zaporozhye	12 Oct. 1949 – 14 Nov. 1955 for both, 20 Dec. 1949 marriage application (with Schmidt Linda daughter of Jacob)
157.	Jungkind, Linda (née Schmidt) dau of Jacob (son born on 26 May 1950)	1930		
158.	Jakovenko, J.A.			Died on 8 Nov. 1949 (death reference attested by Spirov)

Translator's Note: Germans arrived to the Yarnema building column from the town of Onega on October 12, 1949. All of them had their passports issued by the MVD Plesetsk district department on 7 – 22 July and 5 – 8 August 1955. A general date of departure of 14 Nov.1955 is incomprehensible.

*** From Peter Goldade's notes... brother's name was Eugenius*

Book of: "Proceedings of Vologda Society for Northern Region Studies Vologda, 2011" Retrieved by Peter Goldade – U. S. A.
E copy of the book provided by A. Kohler – Ukraine
Hard copy of the book provided by M. Koretnikova - Germany

Translated by: Serge Ant – Odessa, Ukraine